Your New Home

and how to take care of it

Home Builder Press ®
National Association of Home Builders
1201 15th Street, N.W.
Washington, D.C. 20005-2800

Acknowledgment

Home Builder Press® of the National Association of Home Builders expresses its appreciation to the Home Builders Association of Dayton and the Miami Valley for its assistance in preparing this edition.

Your New Home and How to Take Care of It

0-86718-368-3

© 1975, 1978, 1985, 1987, 1988, and 1991
by the Home Builder Press®
of the National Association
of Home Builders of the United States.

Printed in the United States of America

Library of Congress Cataloging-in-Publication Data
Your new home and how to take care of it.
    p.   cm.
   ISBN 0-86718-368-3
   1. Dwellings—Maintenance and repair—Amateurs' manuals.
2. Household appliances—Maintenance and repair—Amateurs'
manuals. I. National Association of Home Builders (U.S.)
TH4817.3.Y68 1991
643'.7—dc20   91-32082
                                                CIP

For further information, please contact:

Home Builder Press®
National Association of Home Builders
1201 15th Street, N.W.
Washington, D.C. 20005-2800
(800) 223-2665

9/91 Merrey/JD Lucas 100M
12/93 HBP/JD Lucas 85M

Contents

Welcome to Your New Home

Your new home was built by a professional builder who used high-quality materials and the latest construction technology. As a member of the National Association of Home Builders, your builder had available the entire resources of one of the nation's largest and most professional trade associations.

More than 3,000 component parts went into your home. Thousands of people had a hand in producing them. Now the components have been assembled into a fine and beautiful house for your enjoyment and comfort.

You should inspect your new home thoroughly before moving in to see that everything has been completed as agreed upon. Make sure that you are satisfied and that the builder's contractual obligations have been met.

If you discover that minor repairs are needed, formally notify the builder in writing—immediately. Telephone calls, oral statements, or messages on scraps of paper can go astray or be forgotten. One way to handle your initial service problems is to make a list of all such items and give it to your builder at the end of a specified period— perhaps 6 weeks after you move in or at some time you have mutually agreed upon. Adverse weather conditions or temporarily unavailable labor or materials may cause a delay in the completion of the jobs on your list. When this happens, your builder will explain the circumstances to you.

The manufacturers and subcontractors who made or installed the various parts and equipment in your house will be responsible for handling some of the service problems that arise while you are living in the house.

Other problems will be your responsibility. This booklet will help you understand what *you* must do to maintain your new home in proper working order and to keep problems to a minimum.

Get to Know Your New Home

This booklet has three purposes:

- ❖ To give a general introduction to the most familiar components of today's new homes.
- ❖ To provide you with basic information needed to care for and maintain your home.
- ❖ To prepare you for the minor adjustments and repairs necessary in most new homes.

Some of the items listed are essential to every home and some are not. For instance, you may or may not have a fireplace, but you certainly will have a heating system and a water supply shut-off valve.

Should your home ever require major repairs, consult your builder for advice or call a specialist in the type of repairs needed. In most cases, major repairs should be left to qualified professionals.

Air-Conditioning Systems

If your home has a central air-conditioning system, the following information can help you get the maximum benefit from it. (See also "Thermostats" under "Heating Systems.")

Registers—The registers throughout your house help to regulate the flow of air and to maintain the desired temperature. By opening and closing the registers and dampers, you can regulate the amount of cool air that enters a room. Once the registers and dampers are adjusted, they will work with the thermostat to maintain the temperature of your home. Closing registers and doors to rooms not in use is a good way to reduce cooling costs. If you have a combined air-conditioning and warm-air heating system, the same registers and dampers will be used to regulate the flow of the heat to the rooms.

In addition to the air outlets, your house will have an air return register. Many houses have more than one.

Neither these nor the other registers should ever be obstructed by furniture, drapes, or other objects.

Filters—Most central air-conditioning systems have an air filter to help keep the air in your home clean. The instruction manual for your cooling system will tell you the location of the filter and how to clean or replace it. (See also "Heating Systems.")

Insulation—Your home has been insulated so that you can regulate the inside temperature in a cost-effective manner. Open doors, windows, and fireplace flues and clogged filters can negate the effects of insulation and cause inadequate cooling (or heating).

Annual Inspection—Like any heating system, a central air-conditioning system should be checked and cleaned periodically by a professional. (See your instruction manual for the frequency of this care.)

Appliances

Your new electric or gas appliances are accompanied by instruction booklets and other papers. Read all instruction literature carefully and remove, fill out, and mail any postcards necessary to record warranties. Keep a list of the authorized service agencies with each instruction booklet.

If an electric appliance fails to operate, be sure it is plugged in before you call a repair service. If the appliance is separately wired, be sure the circuit breaker is on. (See "Circuit Breakers.") If a gas appliance fails to work, check to see if the pilot light is lit. If you suspect a gas leak, turn off the main gas valve near the meter and call the gas company immediately. **Warning:** Do not light matches or smoke cigarettes in the vicinity of the suspected leak.

Attics

Attics, or spaces immediately below roofs, vary in size from crawl spaces to areas large enough to be converted into extra rooms.

Storage—Attic spaces are commonly used for storage, but you should be careful not to put too much strain on your attic floor. Also, attics are susceptible to extremes of heat and cold because attic walls usually are not insulated. Materials stored in attics should not be combustible or perishable under these extreme temperatures.

Insulation—Your home has been constructed to be energy efficient. Occasionally, the insulation on the attic floor may be out of place and leave gaps or block the attic vents. If either of these situations occurs, return the insulation to its proper location. The attic access cover may have insulation attached to the top side. It should also remain securely in place so that no heat is lost through the access hole. Be certain that materials stored in the attic do not compress the insulation because compressed insulation is less effective.

Louvers—Your attic may have louvered openings to allow warm, moist air to escape. Louvered openings should remain unobstructed at all times. If they are closed, harmful quantities of moisture may accumulate.

Bathtubs, Sinks, and Showers

Bathtubs, sinks, and showers are made of a variety of materials. Bathtubs are most frequently made of vitreous china, of porcelain enamel on cast iron or steel, or of fiberglass-reinforced plastic. Bathroom sinks are usually made of vitreous china, of porcelain enamel on cast iron or steel, or of marble resin. Showers are most frequently made of ceramic tile, fiberglass-reinforced plastic, or molded plastic. Kitchen sinks are generally made of porcelain enamel or stainless steel. Laundry tubs or sinks are usually made

of metal or concrete, but fiberglass and plastic are becoming more popular.

To prolong the life of bathtubs and sinks, follow these precautions:

❖ Do not let food wastes stand in the sink. If you have a garbage disposal, dispose of food waste as it accumulates. If you do not have a disposal, put these wastes in an appropriate container.

❖ Do not use bathtubs or sinks to hold paint cans, trash, or tools when you are redecorating; cover bathroom fixtures when painting walls and ceilings.

❖ Do not step in a tub with shoes on for any reason. Shoe soles carry hundreds of gritty particles that will scratch the surface.

❖ Do not use bathtubs or sinks as receptacles for photographic or developing solutions. Developer stains are extremely difficult to remove. (See also "Drains," "Faucets," and "Plumbing.")

By observing these suggestions and using proper cleaning techniques, bathtubs and sinks will retain their newness and luster for many years. However, once damage has occurred, the best plumber in town cannot undo it completely.

Vitreous China and Porcelain Enamel—The surfaces of these fixtures are smooth and glossy like a mirror and harder than steel, but they are not indestructible. Carelessness causes chipping, scratches, and stains. A blow from a heavy or sharp object will chip the surface, and scraping or banging metal utensils will gradually scratch and dull the surface. Shiny new fixtures can also be dulled or stained within a short time through improper or excessive use of strong abrasive cleansers. Most household cleaners are mildly abrasive but are safe if used with plenty of water. A nonabrasive cleaner is safer. If you prefer a dry material, baking soda is nonabrasive.

Food Stains—For most food stains, use a mild solution of chlorine bleach (about 3 tablespoons to a quart of water), and rinse well. For stubborn stains wait 5 minutes before rinsing. (Do not use chlorine bleach on stainless steel.) You can also use a paste of equal parts of cream of tartar, 6 percent hydrogen peroxide, and a household cleaner. Leave paste on stain for 10 to 15 minutes before rinsing.

Cutting food on sink drainboards leaves scratches and nicks. The finish is then susceptible to stains, which become increasingly difficult to remove. (See "Countertops.")

Mildew—Although today's homes are carefully climate controlled, mildew can appear in bathrooms and other areas that collect water vapor—especially in humid regions of the country. An exhaust fan should always be used during baths and showers to help remove water vapor. Wiping condensation from tiles after bathing or showering is a good idea. Damp towels and washcloths should be spread out rather than folded.

To eliminate mildew, clean with a mildew remover (available in nonaerosol spray), rinse, and dry; then use a disinfectant to retard mildew growth and eliminate odor.

Paint—Most oil-based paint will come off easily with turpentine. Water-based paint will come off with a cloth dampened in liquid household cleaner. Small paint spots may be removed by scraping with a razor blade, but you run the risk of gouging the surface. To prevent this damage, be sure the blade is slanted against the fixture. Any residue can be removed with a heavy-duty liquid household cleaner. Rinse thoroughly after using any of these.

Rust Stains—Rust stains are caused mostly by wet metal utensils left on the surface of the sink. Steel wool soap pads also will rust and stain when wet and should be kept in an appropriate container.

Stainless Steel—Stainless steel fixtures generally resist staining and require a thorough scrubbing only occasionally. Use a nonabrasive cleanser or a commercial stainless steel cleanser.

Plastic and Other Substances—Plastic and other substances usually will respond to a nonabrasive cleaner, but the best approach is to check with your plumbing contractor to see what is recommended for the particular material in question. Special commercial cleansers are also available.

Glass Shower Enclosures or Stalls—To clean glass shower enclosures, an ordinary dishwashing detergent (not soap) will do a good job unless hard water minerals have built up. For these use a commercial glass cleaner. **Warning:** Use ample ventilation, avoid breathing the vapor from the spray, and wear rubber gloves.

Caulking—When the caulking around your bathtub or sink dries out or cracks, remove the old caulking and replace it. If you do not have a caulking gun, caulking material can be bought in applicator tubes or in disposable caulking guns. Fill the tub before caulking it.

(See also "Drains.")

Blinds

Before raising venetian blinds, be sure that the slats are in the open position. Blinds may be permanently damaged if they are raised when the slats are closed.

Cleaning—Dust will cause the finish of your blinds to deteriorate. Clean the slats often with a soft cloth. Occasionally the blinds will need to be taken down and washed thoroughly. You should also periodically replace the tapes and cord.

Cabinets

Kitchen and bathroom cabinets (or vanities) should never be cleaned with harsh abrasives. Cabinets made of plastic-coated wood or metal may be cleaned with a detergent solution. Wood cabinets may be cleaned as any other wood furniture unless they are plastic coated. Keep cabinet doors and drawers closed when not in use.

Ceilings

(See "Walls and Ceilings.")

Circuit Breakers

Circuit breakers protect the electrical wiring and equipment in your home from overloading. They are the safety valves of your home's electrical system. Every house should have a master circuit breaker. It generally is located near the smaller circuit breakers. When the master circuit breaker is tripped, the electricity to the house is cut off.

Circuit breakers may be reset by first switching the breaker to full off and then back to full on.

Electrical Service Entrances—The electrical service entrance provides power to the service panel. It has been designed for the electrical needs of the house. Do not tamper with this cable.

Power Failures—In case of a complete power failure, first determine if your neighbors have power. If not, notify the power company. If the power failure affects only your house, check the master switch and circuit breakers. If one circuit breaker continues to trip, check to see if you have overloaded the circuit. If not, call an electrician. Failure to fix a short circuit could result in a fire.

Condensation

(See "Foundations" and "Walls and Ceilings.")

Countertops

Countertops are generally heat and stain resistant under proper care, but they should be protected from hot irons as well as pots, pans, or baking dishes taken directly from an oven, broiler, or burner. Never cut anything directly on the countertop because the knife may dent or nick the surface. Countertops made of plastic-coated wood or metal may be cleaned with a detergent solution.

According to the manufacturer, most stains wipe off of Corian because it is not porous. Stubborn stains and cigarette burns can be rubbed off with abrasive household cleanser or fine sandpaper.

If any of your countertop or work surface is unfinished wood, it will require special care. To protect it from spills, coat it lightly with olive oil (including the edges), let the oil soak in for a few minutes, and then rub it dry with a soft lintless cloth. Several thin coats will provide better protection than one heavy coat. To remove onion, garlic, or other odors, rub the surface with a slice of citrus fruit (lemon, orange, etc.), sprinkle lightly with salt, and wipe immediately with a soft cloth or paper towel. Clean it with a mild chlorine bleach solution once a week and also after cutting raw meat on it. Rinse thoroughly and wipe dry. If you do not have a built-in chopping block, buy a portable cutting board to protect your countertops and drainboards.

Because marble is easily stained or etched, it should be protected according to the manufacturer's instructions. Compatible sealing, polishing, and cleaning products are available from suppliers of marble and from some hardware stores.

Decks

Decks have become a highly desirable feature for outdoor enjoyment. The wood used in decks usually is pressurized and treated, but decks generally require some mainte-

nance to protect them from moisture. After the moisture from the treatment dries out and periodically thereafter, pressure-treated wood decks should have a coat of water repellent and preservative. Follow the supplier's recommendations. Over time a floor board may warp, causing a nail to pop up. Replace the floor board if needed.

Disposals

If you have a garbage disposal, it will probably be one of two types: continuous feed or batch feed with locking cover. The instruction booklet will give precise directions for disposal operation. Always use cold water when the disposal is on and especially when grinding greasy substances. Many people erroneously conclude that because their waste disposal is capable of grinding up most of their garbage, it is also capable of eliminating grease and other substances they would not otherwise pour down a drain. In fact, you should be equally careful not to clog disposal drains with grease. Should the drain become clogged, do not put chemicals down the disposal. (See also "Drains.")

Avoid putting large amounts of fibrous materials (such as banana peels or corn husks) down your disposal. Also avoid grinding bones or other hard materials.

Reset Buttons—Most disposals have a reset button that works in much the same way as a circuit breaker. Should the disposal become overloaded with a substance it cannot grind, it will turn itself off. If this happens, turn the switch off, remove the substance obstructing the disposal's operation, wait about 3 minutes, and push the reset button. (See your instruction booklet for its location.) Turn the switch on; if it still does not start, turn if off again and check to see if you have tripped the circuit breaker. If the circuit breaker has not interrupted the flow of the current, turn off the circuit breaker and use a mop or broom handle to turn the rotating plate in the disposal unit until it turns freely. Restore current, push the reset button again, and turn the disposal switch on. Some disposals come

15

equipped with a special wrench that can be inserted in a hole in the bottom of the disposal (under the sink). Others have a two-pronged wrench that fits into the top of the rotating plate. Turning the wrench a couple of times will usually loosen the material enough so that the disposal will start. **Warning:** Be absolutely sure the circuit breaker is off before inserting tongs to remove material when the disposal is stalled. Also be sure it is off before using the wrench or a broomstick.

Doors

Sticking—Sticking is the most common problem with doors. If the sticking is caused by swelling in damp weather, fold sandpaper around a wooden block and sand the edge that binds. If the hinge screws are loose, tighten them, and if the door is still out of alignment, sand or plane the edge that binds. Always paint or varnish areas that have been sanded or planed. Paint and varnish protect wood from moisture and help to prevent further door problems.

Warping—Warping is another result of too much moisture. If a door warps, the best remedy is to dry it in the sun. If the door is still warped after being thoroughly dried, apply weights to the bulged side and leave it for 2 or 3 days.

Storm Doors—A storm door may reduce your heating costs. Storm doors are usually made of aluminum, wood, vinyl-clad wood, or solid vinyl. Houses with insulated steel exterior doors do not need separate storm doors. In mild climates, storm doors are unnecessary.

Weatherstripping—To maintain your home's energy efficiency, exterior doors come equipped with weatherstripping made from a variety of materials, including metal, plastic, and rubber. This weatherstripping must remain properly in place to prevent the loss of expensively conditioned air or infiltration of outside air. Metal weatherstripping may need to be renailed if it becomes loose, bent out away from the edge of the door, or does not seal tightly when the door is closed. This repair is a simple process that requires only a hammer or pliers.

For rubber or plastic weatherstripping, regluing or renailing should be all that is necessary. For regluing, use a strong, water-resistant household glue. Do not use a cyanoacrylic (super) glue.

Painting—Wood exterior doors should be painted when the house or trim is painted usually every 4 to 6 years. Varnished doors may need to be recoated more often. Aluminum, vinyl-clad wood, and solid vinyl doors do not need to be painted. Painted doors may be cleaned with a mild detergent; polyurethane varnish would require a damp cloth. Other types of varnish should be cleaned like good furniture. (For care and cleaning of the glass in doors, see "Windows.")

Garage Doors—The moving parts of garage doors should be oiled every 3 months. The screws that fasten the hardware to a wood door should be tightened every 12 months because the wood shrinks a little as it ages, and the screws may loosen. If a hinged, wooden door sags, tightening the appropriate turnbuckle should bring it back into shape. Each garage door usually has two of these, one on each of two cables crisscrossing the back of the door. An overhead door may warp inward from being left up for long periods. Usually this warp can be corrected by adjusting the nuts on the metal rods or the straps across the top and bottom of the door. Sliding garage doors that drag can be realigned by tightening the bolts on the wheels that run on the overhead track. Also, check that the floor guide is not out of line.

Locks—If the security of your home is a concern, consider these items before installing additional locks in your doors:

- Locks should be located so that they cannot be reached by breaking a small windowpane in the door.
- Locks that require a key on the inside are potentially dangerous if an emergency occurs. When this type of lock is used, be sure a spare key is always handy to prevent anyone from being trapped inside the house.
- Installation of any locks or chains will be most secure if the screws and bolts used for attachment go all the way through the door or frame and cannot be removed from the outside.
- A metal insulated door may require the services of an expert to properly install new locks. (See also "Security Systems.")

Drains

Each plumbing fixture in your house has a drain trap. This ∩-shaped piece of pipe is designed to provide a water barrier that prevents the airborne bacteria and odor of sewer gas from entering the house. Any fixture that is used infrequently (such as a basement shower) should be turned on at regular intervals to replace evaporated water and ensure that the barrier remains intact. Because of their shape, traps are also the source of most clogging problems.

Bathtubs, Sinks, and Showers—When the drain pipe from a tub, sink, or shower becomes clogged, use a plunger first. The rubber cup of the plunger should cover the drain opening, and the water should come well up over the cup edge. Working the plunger up and down rhythmically 10 to 20 times in succession will build up pressure in the pipe and do more good than sporadic plunges. Plug any overflow outlet with a piece of old cloth. When working on a double sink, be sure to close the other drain.

If the plunger does not work, use a plumber's snake. You can rent or purchase one at a hardware or plumbing store. Turn the handle of the snake in the same direction when removing it as you did when inserting it. This technique will keep anything attached to the snake from coming loose before it is removed.

If the drain can be partly opened with the plunger or snake, boiling water (140° F for plastic pipes) may complete the job. If not, you can open the trap under the fixture. (Access to a tub or shower trap is usually gained through a small panel in an adjoining closet wall or floor.) Put a bucket or pan under the trap to catch the water in it. A piece of wire may help to dislodge the blockage. The snake can also be run at this point.

Although it is sold commercially as drain cleaner, never use caustic soda to open a drain. It will combine with the grease from the soap or food wastes to form an insoluble compound.

Toilets—A clogged toilet should be treated almost the same way as a clogged drain. The trap is built into the toilet and is therefore less accessible. Instead of a snake, use a coil spring-steel auger, which can be bought or rented from a hardware or plumbing store. Insert the auger so that the point goes up into the trap. Turning the handle of the auger will break up the blockage or catch it so that it can be removed. An auger is easier to use if one person holds it while another turns the handle.

Prevention—Ordinary washing soda (not baking soda) added to a drain on a regular basis will help to keep it clear of the grease from soap and cooking utensils. Run hot water through the drain, turn off the water, add 3 tablespoons of washing soda, and follow it with just enough hot water to wash it down the drain opening. Let stand for 15 minutes and run more hot water. To avoid clogging drains or toilets, never pour grease into them. (See also "Plumbing," "Toilets," and "Bathtubs, Sinks, and Showers.")

Driveways, Walks, and Steps

Various materials are used for driveways, walks, and steps. Concrete and asphalt are most common for driveways. Walks and steps are usually concrete, but they may be made of brick or other material.

Concrete—Your builder has anticipated stresses on concrete driveways, walks, and steps and has provided contraction and expansion joints to minimize cracking. However, cracking is one of the characteristics of concrete, and a method of entirely eliminating cracks has not been discovered yet. Unanticipated cracking sometimes occurs from unforeseeable conditions, such as severe frost. Ordinarily, the cracks are of no serious consequence.

Cracks—Minor repairs can be made by following these steps:

❖ Roughen the edges of the crack if they are smooth.
❖ Clean out loose material and dirt.
❖ Soak the old concrete thoroughly. The crack should be sopping wet, but water should not be standing in it.

❖ Fill the crack with patching cement slightly higher than the crack to allow for shrinkage. Commercially prepared patching mixtures need only the addition of water, but be sure the mixture you buy is appropriate for concrete.

❖ Cover the patch and keep it damp for several days. The longer the drying time, the stronger the patch will be.

❖ When the cement has partly set, remove excess cement with a wire brush. At this stage the surface of the cement appears sandy.

Asphalt—Oil, gasoline, or similar substances can cause serious damage if dropped or spilled on a blacktopped driveway, walkway, or parking area. Wash it off immediately with sudsy water and then rinse. Do not let sharp objects such as outdoor furniture legs and bicycle stands rest on the asphalt because they will poke holes in it. Never burn leaves or anything else on your driveway or parking area.

Brick—(See "Exterior Brick Walls" under "Walls and Ceilings.")

Winter Safety—Protect your driveways, walks, and steps by removing snow and ice promptly. If a thin layer of ice cannot be removed, use cat litter or sand for traction. They are safe for driveways, walks, steps, and nearby grass or shrubs. Do not apply salt in any form. Repeated thaw and freezing with salt and chemicals can damage concrete, brick, mortar, and asphalt, and salt will kill grass, shrubs, and trees. Provide an outdoor floor mat to prevent the cat litter or sand from being tracked into the house. Another mat just inside the door will provide additional protection for carpets and floors.

Electrical Receptacles

The wiring in your new home meets the code requirements and safety standards for the normal use of electrical appliances. Ordinarily, small appliances that require personal attendance for their operation may be plugged into any electrical receptacle without fear of overloading a circuit. However, the use of a large appliance or of many small appliances on the same circuit may cause an overload. If a circuit breaker trips frequently, contact a licensed electrical contractor to learn whether additional wiring is needed. (See "Circuit Breakers.")

Faucets

The faucets in your home will sometimes require repair. The less strain you put on faucets, the less frequently they will need repair.

Aerators—Cleaning the aerators will be your most frequent task in maintaining faucets. An aerator adds air to the water as it leaves the faucet and eliminates splashing. It also reduces water usage, thereby saving you money. Aerators are most common on kitchen faucets, but they are also used for bathroom sinks. To clean an aerator, unscrew it from the mouth of the faucet, remove any deposits, remove and rinse the washers and screens, replace them in their original order, and put the aerator back on the faucet. The frequency of the need for cleaning will depend on the condition of the water, but generally every 3 or 4 months is adequate.

Leaks—All leaks raise your water bill, and a leaking outside faucet can cause a damp basement. Inside or outside, leaking faucets generally can be fixed by replacing the washers. Some faucets with single controls for hot and cold water have no washers, but their cartridges, which last longer than washers, must still be changed periodically. Before attempting to repair a faucet, turn off the water at the nearest intake valve. Washers may be obtained at most hardware stores. For cartridges, you may have to go to a plumbing store.

Outside Faucets—If the temperature falls below freezing in the winter and frostproof fittings are not provided, outside water connections for summer gardening should be turned off and inside and outside pipes drained before cold weather begins. This precaution will prevent the freezing and bursting of the outside pipes and fittings. The control valve is usually inside the house close to where the water supply goes through the exterior wall. Open the outside faucet to drain off any excess water. Remove the garden hose and store it for the duration of the cold weather.

Fireplaces

Before using your fireplace, equip it with andirons (or a grate) and a well-fitting screen, and check to see if it draws properly. To do this, open the damper, light a newspaper on the andirons or grate and see if the smoke is carried up

the chimney. Before lighting any fire, the damper should be opened. Keep the damper closed when the fireplace is not in use so that warm air will not escape in the winter and cool air will not escape in the summer. Build any fire on the andirons or grate—not directly on the fireplace floor. Do not burn trash or rubbish in the fireplace. Never use kerosene, gasoline, or other highly flammable liquids to start a fire, and always be sure the fire is out each night before you retire. Store firewood outside away from the house because it may harbor insects and because wood stored outside will burn longer.

Cleaning—Occasionally throwing a handful of salt on the fire will help prevent the accumulation of soot, and it will also add color to the flames. However, salt should never be used in fireplaces made of metal. The chimney should be checked periodically to see if cleaning is necessary. A chimney professional can tell you if your chimney needs cleaning.

Floors

Floors are usually made of either concrete or wood, and covered by a wide variety of materials.

Concrete Floors—Concrete floors are generally mainte-nance free, but they are susceptible to cracking under unusual conditions. (For repair of such cracks see "Drive-ways, Walks, and Steps" and "Foundations.") Occasion-ally basement floors will collect water from condensation of moisture in the air on cold basement walls. (For treat-ment of this condition, see "Foundations.")

A concrete sealer will make an unpainted concrete floor easier to keep clean. Follow the manufacturer's directions for cleaning after the sealer has been applied. Unpainted concrete floors should not be cleaned with soap. Instead, use a solution of 4 to 6 tablespoons of washing soda to a gallon of hot water. First, wet the floor with clear water. If necessary, scouring powder may be used in conjunction with the washing soda solution. A stiff brush will help to loosen dirt. Rinse with clear water. Painted concrete floors can be cleaned with plain water or a mild soap or detergent solution.

Hardwood Floors—The structural lumber in your house has been selected in sizes and grades to provide a safety factor well beyond what is required to carry the load. Some shrinkage may occur in these framing members, but your home has been designed so that any settling will be as even as possible.

As with other building materials, wood may contract or expand with weather changes. It is not affected by heat or cold, but it may shrink under extreme dryness or swell under extreme humidity.

The hardwood floors in your new home have been precision manufactured and expertly installed and finished by skilled craftspeople. Normal maintenance should include regular vacuuming or dry mopping to remove surface dust and dirt. If your floors have a polyurethane finish you should vacuum them regularly and wipe them occasionally with a damp (not wet) mop or cloth. Do not use water on hardwood floors finished with anything other than polyurethane. Water sometimes causes the grain to rise, and prolonged use may cause cracks from the expansion and shrinkage of the wood.

Hardwood floors with other finishes probably will need to be waxed periodically. The frequency of cleaning and waxing depends on the amount of traffic they receive. Always use a "spirit" wax, either liquid or paste. The wax can be buffed most easily with an electric polisher that can usually be rented at a neighborhood hardware store or supermarket. If you use a "self-polishing" liquid wax, be sure it is made for use on hardwood floors.

On moderately soiled floors where traffic is not excessive, cleaning and polishing can be done in one operation with clean-and-wax products. To use these, remove black marks with dry steel wool, sweep or dry mop to remove loose dirt, and apply the clean-and-wax product according to the manufacturer's directions. Rinse the applicator in water to remove any soil. If floors become excessively soiled, they can be cleaned with mineral spirits or commercial cleaners that leave a protective coat of wax as they clean.

When applying wax or cleaner, keep it away from baseboards—little traffic occurs there. This practice will minimize the build-up of wax and extend the periods between removal.

Protect the finish on the floors by attaching furniture rests to the bottom of furniture legs. They also help to distribute the weight better.

Resilient Floors—Resilient floors include linoleum, asphalt, and rubber. For daily care, remove loose dirt with a broom, dust mop, or vacuum. Wipe up spills immediately, but if a spill or spot dries, remove it with a damp sponge, cloth, or mop.

To prolong the period between cleanings, occasionally wipe resilient floors with a damp mop. When floors are dull or cannot be refurbished by mopping, clean them thoroughly with a good detergent, diluted as recommended by the floor manufacturer. Use just enough mechanical action with a mop, cloth, or floor scrubber to loosen dirt. Remove the cleaning solution, rinse the floor, and let it dry. Some resilient floors are designed to never need waxing, but some of them require a coat of floor polish. Your flooring contractor can tell you what kind of flooring you have.

The best polish for most resilient floors is water emulsion wax. Apply either the wax or a floor finish to a clean dry floor. The finishes provide hard films that do not smear but also do not respond to buffing. Waxy polishes leave softer films with slightly lower gloss that can be buffed to restore a shiny appearance. Apply the polish sparingly—use the least amount that can be applied without streaking. Let it dry about 30 minutes before allowing anyone to walk on it. Some porous floors may require two coats, with a buffing after each. About once or twice a year, take off built-up old polish or wax with remover. Dilute it as recommended, apply, rinse, let it dry, and apply a new coat of polish.

Tile Floors—Ceramic tile normally needs only a wipe with a damp cloth or an occasional wet mopping to stay clean and new looking. If necessary, a more thorough cleaning with a detergent or ceramic tile cleaner will remove grime.

To remove particularly heavy accumulations of film from glazed tile, you may need a stiff brush and mild scouring powder. Unglazed tile may be scrubbed or scraped. To clean the joints between tiles, use a fiber brush and a mild cleanser. A special sealer for grout will make it more stain resistant. Staining agents should be mopped up promptly. Even though they rarely affect ceramic tile, they may stain the grout.

Cork Floors—Use a spirit wax or wax cleaner on cork tile. Minor stains can be sanded out with fine grade sandpaper. Rewax after sanding the stain. Cork floors may need two coats of wax with a buffing after each. Epoxy-coated cork floors are stain resistant.

Slate Floors—Use a sealer on the slate and then clean it with a mild detergent solution.

Marble Floors—(See care of marble at the end of "Countertops.")

Foundations

The weight of your house rests upon the foundation. The foundation consists of the footing—a large mass of concrete poured into a trench—and the foundation walls, which rest on the footing. Foundation walls are usually made of poured concrete, masonry block, or wood framing. If you have a basement, the foundation walls also serve as the basement walls.

Foundation walls are subject to a wide variety of stresses and strains. Because the base of the wall is in the ground, it maintains a fairly constant temperature. However, the top portion extends out of the ground and may be subject to extreme seasonal temperature changes. The changes cause concrete and masonry to expand and contract.

Cracks—Combinations of stresses and temperature variations may cause cracks in the basement or foundation walls. These cracks do not affect the strength of the structures and may be easily repaired if desired.

To fill medium to large cracks:

❖ Roughen the edge of the crack if it is smooth. For large cracks, undercut the crack to form a V-shaped groove to a depth about equal to the width of the crack at the surface.

❖ Clean out all loose particles of cement, mortar, or concrete with a wire brush or a thin blade.

❖ Wet the crack thoroughly.

❖ Fill the crack with patching cement, allowing a little extra for shrinkage. Be sure the patching mixture is suitable for the job.

❖ Just before the cement hardens, rub it with burlap or a similar material to give it a texture similar to that of the wall. Wetting a trowel before going over the patch for the last time will produce a smooth surface.

❖ Paint it to match the rest of the wall if necessary. To repair small cracks, fill them with a heavy paste made by mixing dry cement-base paint with a little water. Force the paste into the crack with a stiff bristle brush or putty knife. To match the existing wall finish, use a colored paint to form the paste. In lieu of cement-base paint, you may use a mixture of cement and fine sand (one part cement, two parts sand capable of passing through a 100-mesh screen) mixed with sufficient water to form a heavy paste.

For the fine or hairline cracks, work cement-base paint into the crack with a short, stiff bristle brush.

Condensation—Probably the most disturbing problem in a new home is condensation. It may look as if moisture is seeping through basement walls, pipes are leaking, or water is coming through the windows. Condensation takes place wherever warm, moist air inside the house comes in contact with a colder surface, such as a window, basement wall, or an exposed pipe. Actually, a perfectly dry basement can have wet walls because moisture in the air condenses on cold basement walls during the summer months. Windows should be closed during damp, humid weather and opened during clear, dry weather.

Condensation is at its maximum in new homes. When your home was new, gallons of water went into the concrete of your basement wall. This water comes out of the walls by evaporation, which consequently raises the moisture content above normal. Proper ventilation will bring this normal drying-out process to its conclusion as steadily as possible. However, do not try to speed up the process by creating extremely high temperatures during the winter. The house will dry out unevenly, which will exaggerate the effects of normal shrinkage.

Condensation also may be reduced by providing outside vents for equipment such as a clothes dryer. Some warm-air furnaces have humidifiers to bring moisture content in the air up to healthy standards during winter months. If excessive humidity develops, turn the humidifier down or off to prevent excess water vapor.

Some houses are equipped with fans in the kitchen, bath, or utility areas that exhaust moist air and odors to the outside. If your house has such fans, use them for short periods of time when excessive moisture is being generated. Turn these fans off as soon as possible because they exhaust expensively conditioned air, either warm or cool, to the outside.

Leaks—As with all the other parts of your house, basement walls are not waterproof themselves. Where conditions have warranted, the builder has damp-proofed the underground portions of the foundation to prevent the entrance of water from surrounding soil.

Repair of basement leaks depends upon local conditions that make each case different. Before making extensive or expensive structural repairs to correct wet-wall conditions, thoroughly check your drainage system. In many instances, repairing or adjusting downspouts or gutters will help to carry surface water away from foundation walls.

If the ground outside your basement slopes toward the wall, pack and bank up soil so that water will drain away. Avoid planting shrubbery within less than 3 feet of the foundation. Never water your plants toward the foundation. (See also "Landscaping.")

Furnaces

(See "Heating Systems.")

Gutters and Downspouts

Always keep gutters and downspouts unobstructed by leaves, tree limbs, or anything that could cause overflowing. Vinyl gutters never need to be painted. Aluminum gutters need not be painted, but can be if you choose. Gutters made of most other metals will need a coat of rust-retardant paint whenever the rest of the house is painted (every 4 to 6 years). Be sure that downspouts direct water away from the foundation.

Heating Systems

Heating systems, methods, and installations vary widely. The capacity of the system in your home has been determined by the heating load necessary to keep your home at a comfortable temperature. Oversized systems are inefficient. Learn everything you can about the system installed in your home: how it operates, how it functions at maximum efficiency, and what kind of fuel it uses. If you have any questions after studying the instruction manual for your heating system, your heating contractor can probably provide the answers. Never burn rubbish or anything but the designated fuel in the heating system.

Thermostats—The thermostat (usually located on an inside wall) helps to keep your entire house at a comfortable temperature. Individual room temperatures may be further regulated by adjusting the registers in the various rooms or the dampers in the ducts from the furnace to the registers. If your home is heated by a warm-air system, your thermostat may also contain controls for converting the heating system to the cooling system.

You can significantly reduce your heating bill by lowering the thermostat during the sleeping hours and when your home will be unoccupied for a prolonged period. Some homes are equipped with set-back thermostats that can automatically reduce the setting shortly before bedtime and return it to normal prior to morning or wake-up.

Because of the special characteristics of heat pumps, a constant setting on the thermostat is recommended. Do not use an automatic set-back thermostat with a heat pump and do not set back the heat manually.

Maintenance—The controls on all types of heating systems occasionally malfunction. Such a problem does not mean that anything is fundamentally wrong with the system. Usually a simple adjustment will solve the problem, but unless you are trained to make such adjustments, you should rely on the skills of a professional. Also call on a professional for an annual inspection and cleaning of your heating system. The best time to do this work is late summer or early autumn.

Filters—Some types of warm-air furnaces have filters, usually found near where the cooled air returns from other rooms. These filters remove dirt and dust from the air. For efficient heating, they should be replaced at least every 3 months during each heating season. In some areas more frequent changing may be desirable. If you cannot see through the filter held up to a light, it needs to be changed. Usually, replacement consists of removing one or two metal screws, pulling out the dirty filter, and inserting a new one obtained from a hardware or department store. With some furnaces you need only open a latch to get to the filter. Some heating systems require two filters stacked vertically; for this type, both filters should be changed at the same time. Read the instruction booklet for your heating system for specific directions. Radiant-type heating systems do not have filters.

Humidifiers—If your furnace has a humidifying attachment, it will be one of two types: power or evaporative. Both types will need occasional cleaning to remove accumulated mineral deposits that can interfere with proper functioning.

Oiling—Forced warm-air heating systems contain an electric motor and fan within the furnace enclosure. Some of these systems require oiling at the beginning of and during the heating season. Front or side panels generally can be removed so that you can reach the fan and the electric motor as well as the oil cups. (See the instruction booklet for specific directions.)

Pilot Lights—Keep the pilot light of a gas-fired furnace burning during the summer; the extremely small amount of heat it generates will keep the furnace dry and prevent corrosion. The furnace will be ready for the first cold snap of the autumn. However, you need not keep it lighted if you have a combined heating and cooling system. Some models now have pilotless ignitions, which save energy and require less attention.

Hot Water Heating System—With a hot water system, water is heated to about 180° F by the water heater and forced through the pipes by a small pump called a circulator.

Hot water heat is generally of two types: radiant and radiant-convection. In the radiant type the hot water pipes may be in the ceiling, walls, or floors, but they most commonly run through baseboard panels on the outside walls of the rooms. The baseboard heats the wall to about 5 feet above the floor, and the wall itself serves as a radiation panel.

In the radiant-convection type, the hot water runs through fine copper pipes behind baseboard panels with openings in the top and bottom to allow the cold air to enter, pass over the fins, and rise when it is warmed. Some manufacturers make the two types of heating panels in matching units so they can be interlocked and used together.

Electric Heating System—With radiant electric heat, an electric cable provides the source of radiation. As with hot water pipes, the cable may be installed in walls, ceilings, and floors, but it is generally in a decorative baseboard panel.

Insulation—(See "Air-Conditioning Systems.")

Reducing Utility Bills—Your household's lifestyle is the largest single variable that affects your utility bills. Identical homes on the same street may have utility bills that vary by 100 percent. By living "smarter" in your new home, you can maximize the benefits from insulation and other energy saving features your builder has installed.

Common sense activities—such as those that follow—can produce substantial savings:

❖ Closing the windows and doors when the heating/cooling system is working

- ❖ Not running the dryer, stove, or oven on a hot summer day
- ❖ Adjusting thermostat settings to 68° F (or lower) in the winter and to 75° F (or higher) in the summer
- ❖ Closing the drapes or curtains on hot days when the sun shines into your home

Think about the way you live in your home and look for ways to improve the efficiency of all the systems. Remember that in the summer, part of the heat removed from the home by the air-conditioning system is generated inside by lights, appliances, and people. Also, during the heating season, the sun can warm the inside of the house even on cold days and take part of the load off the furnace if you open drapes on the sunny side of the house.

During winter vacations, do not shut off the heat or you may come home and find a frozen or burst pipe.

Hoods

(See "Ranges, Ovens, and Broilers.")

Landscaping

Proper care of the grounds around your house can not only add to its beauty but also protect the structure of the house.

Grading—Drainage swales or other discharge channels were sized and sloped to accommodate the water runoff and should be kept clear of debris such as leaves, gravel, and trash. Allow 6 inches of clearance between your grading and the wall siding; otherwise, water may enter the joint between the foundation and the wall material, or the wood may decay. As the earth around the house becomes compacted, depressions may form. These places must be filled with dirt so that water will not form puddles in them or cause dampness.

Lawn and Plants—Water your new lawn and shrubs often. In the fall of the first year rake the lawn thoroughly, reseed it, and add organic fertilizer or manure. Give special attention to bare spots. When watering the lawn, avoid sprinkling painted parts of the house, which can reduce the life expectancy of the paint. If you plant flower beds near the house, do not disturb the earth next to the foundation. Always dig the beds several feet away.

The Landscaping Plan—Plan your landscaping according to how you want your grounds to look in 10 years. Long-range planning takes more time, but it pays off.

Before you dig a single hole, you need reliable, specific information about the local flora and its requirements. Then you can decide what to plant, where to plant it, and how much of a budget you need.

As you learn about plants, remember that the landscaping around your house is an extension of the indoor living space. The grounds should include defined areas for work and play, often best screened or partitioned by trees, shrubs, or other greenery.

You will probably want plants of various sizes and shapes that attract the eye both near and far. You will need taller shrubs for privacy, trees for shade, flowering trees for color, low-growing plants under windows, and thicker evergreens for backgrounds.

The beauty of having a landscape plan is that you need not feel compelled to carry out the plan all at once. You can work it out a little at a time, as gradually or as rapidly as time and money allow, yet still know where you are going at every step.

Once you have a general plan in mind, list all the plants that appeal to you, then see what your garden encyclopedia and other references say about them.

When you start the actual design, make a sketch of your property to scale. Carefully plot the exact location of the house, walks, walls, trees, and any other landscape features. Indicate doors and windows too because they will influence the location of plants.

Sketch in the areas you want to reserve for turf, and precisely locate each shrub and tree that you have chosen to plant. Try to figure their space requirements at maturity, particularly if you expect to plant young stock. And take care not to plant anything that will grow up to block a good view or shut out light needed at a window.

If all this sounds like a lot of work, remember that a thoughtful plan minimizes wasted effort in the long run. You should make a long-range plan, stick with it, and make changes only if they improve the overall scheme. The period when everything seems barely a foot high will pass soon enough. Before you know it, your landscaping will be the envy of the neighborhood. It could increase the value of the property.

Louvers

(See "Attics.")

Microwave Ovens

(See "Ranges, Ovens, and Broilers.")

Mildew

(See "Bathtubs, Sinks, and Showers.")

Moldings

(See "Trimmings and Moldings.")

Motors

Many heavy-duty appliances such as refrigerators, air-conditioners, washing machines, dryers, dishwashers, etc., have motors that require periodic servicing. Consult your appliance manual for information about the care of these motors.

Plumbing

The plumbing in your house was installed by a professional and generally should need only minimum maintenance if you care for it properly. If any problem arises, attend to it promptly to prevent a bigger and often more costly problem.

Intake Valves—All members of your household should become familiar with the various water intake valves in your plumbing system. Label each one with a shipping or luggage tag. You will rarely need to use them, but in the event of an emergency or if you need to make minor repairs, they will be easy to locate. Intake valves for toilets are usually under the water chamber. Those for sinks are usually under the sink, while the main intake valve is usually near the point at which the water enters the house.

Leaks—Copper pipes should last the lifetime of a house, but if a joint should loosen, it will need to be resoldered—

a job requiring an acetylene torch and best left to a plumber. Plastic pipe should also last the lifetime of the house, and a loose joint should likewise be repaired by a plumber.

If your washing machine, dishwasher, or other water-using appliance appears to leak, first check to see that the trap through which it drains is completely open. Sometimes a partially clogged drain can cause an overflow within the appliance. (See also "Drains.")

Noisy Pipes—Pipes make noise for a variety of reasons. Among the most common are a worn washer, a loose part in a faucet, or steam in a hot water pipe. The condition causing noisy pipes should be corrected promptly because sometimes the noise is accompanied by vibration. A strong vibration can cause fittings to loosen and leak. (See also "Bathtubs, Sinks, and Showers," "Drains," "Faucets," and "Water Heaters.")

Frozen Pipes—To prevent pipes from freezing, never leave a house unheated during cold weather. During an extended period of severe cold, provide at least a little heat for unused rooms and baths that are not generally heated. Ordinary antifreeze will provide protection for toilets and drain pipes, but it cannot be used in the water distribution pipes. In cold climates, be sure all entrances to crawl spaces are closed during cold weather.

If a pipe should freeze, proper defrosting may prevent damage. The pipe must be thawed slowly to prevent the formation of steam, which could cause it to burst. You should first restore heat to the affected part of the house. A frozen pipe is most likely to be on an outside wall exposed to winter winds. Open all faucets connected to the lines so that steam can escape if any forms during thawing. Begin the thaw at the frozen point nearest the faucet. A thermometer held against an exposed pipe helps to locate this point.

A heat lamp set at least 6 inches from a plasterboard or panel-type wall will thaw the pipes behind it. In some houses the baseboard panel can be removed and the nozzle of a hair dryer inserted with the warm air directed parallel to the pipes. A hair dryer or heat lamp is also suitable for defrosting exposed pipes. Again the air from the hair dryer should be directed parallel to the pipes. A soldering iron or a regular clothes iron set on warm may be strapped to an exposed pipe for safe thawing, but be sure that the iron touches only the pipe. As the pipe thaws, move the source of heat toward the frozen area until the job is complete. If a sink trap is involved, boiling water poured into it may solve the problem. Small cooking appliances can be set under exposed horizontal pipes, but be sure the appliances do not touch the pipe. If a large amount of pipe is involved or if an underground pipe is frozen, call a plumber. Plumbers have equipment for thawing pipes electrically.

Ranges, Ovens, and Broilers

Many ovens and broilers, both built-in and floor models, have self-cleaning cycles or clean themselves as they are used. Others must be cleaned in the conventional manner. The outside of your stove, oven, or broiler can be cleaned with a nonabrasive cleaner such as baking soda sprinkled on a damp cloth or sponge. Or the manufacturer may make a special appliance cleaner that both cleans and protects against stains. If your burner panel or oven front is stainless steel, you may want to use a stainless steel cleaner on it. Never use harsh, abrasive cleaners on the outside of stoves, ovens, or broilers.

Do not let the oven go too long between cleanings. A lightly soiled oven can be cleaned with a solution of ¼ cup baking soda to 1 quart of water. Rubbing with a paste of baking soda and water may be necessary for some spots. A heavily soiled oven may require a commercial oven cleaner. Choose one that is noncorrosive and nontoxic and follow directions and cautions closely.

Electric—An electric stove will usually have a separate circuit. If your range fails to work, check the proper circuitry. (See "Circuit Breakers.")

Gas—If the burners of your stove, oven, or broiler fail to light, check to see that the pilot light is lit. If it is, the burners may be clogged and should be cleaned. If they are removable, the burners can be soaked clean in a solution of washing soda, but do not soak them in an aluminum pan. A wire brush or thin stiff wire may be helpful in removing burned food particles from the holes in the gas burners. When using wire, be careful not to push the material farther into the holes. If you suspect that gas is leaking, turn off the main valve (near the meter) and call the gas company immediately. **Warning:** Do not light matches or smoke.

Hoods—The filters in range hoods need to be cleaned or changed periodically. For location and directions, consult your instruction manual. Fan motors should be oiled periodically.

Microwave Ovens—Follow owner's instruction booklet for safety and use. Because some containers and utensils can permanently damage microwave ovens, make sure that the ones you use in your oven are safe for microwaving.

You can remove some spatters and drips from the oven's interior with a damp cloth. Greasy spatters require a sudsy cloth and rinse. A cloth dampened in a solution of baking soda is also safe, but never use a commercial oven cleaner on any part of your microwave oven. Do not use abrasives such as cleaning powders or steel or plastic pads on any part of your microwave oven. They will mar the surface.

For exterior maintenance, wipe the case and control panel with a damp cloth and dry thoroughly. Do not use cleaning sprays, large amounts of soap and water, abrasives, or sharp objects on the panel.

Registers

(See "Air-Conditioning Systems.")

Roofs

Your roof will give you many years of good service if it is properly maintained. Flashing seals those places where the roof abuts walls, chimneys, dormers, or valleys where two roof slopes meet. If a leak should occur, call a qualified roofer to make the repair. A qualified roofer should inspect the roof at least every 3 years. If you have to walk on the roof for any reason, be careful not to damage the surface or the flashing. Be particularly careful when installing a TV or radio antenna—a careless job can cause serious leaks.

Freeze–Thaw Cycles—Winter storms followed by relatively mild temperatures cause freeze–thaw cycles that can create leaks in roofs.

Most roof shingling is not waterproof. Shingles are meant to shed water down their overlapping courses into gutters or off the roof overhang. Erratic weather conditions can cause a build-up of water—from snow or ice dams formed either on the roof or in gutters and downspouts. This water backs up under the shingles or eventually seeps through the shingles, causing leaks.

Although roofs with a shallow pitch are more susceptible to this phenomenon than are steeply pitched roofs, no conventional home is completely immune to the problem. Remove ice blockades from gutters and downspouts, and attempt to remove built-up ice and snow from the lower portions of the roof. In areas of the country where freeze–thaw cycles are prevalent, some homeowners lay heating cables in their gutters and even part of the way up the roof to counteract the freezing process. (See also "Gutters.")

Screens

(See "Windows.")

Security Systems

Although security systems are installed to work autonomously, you should regularly (a) check that the alarm and circuits are in working order and (b) inspect sensors one by one. Consult your instruction manual on how to inspect the sensors. Check any primary and backup batteries once a month, and replace them at least once a year.

Septic Tanks

All septic tank installations must meet local health standards. With proper care and attention, septic tanks will serve as satisfactorily as sewers. Otherwise, they can become a burdensome expense and, when functioning improperly, a neighborhood health menace.

Learn the location of the septic tank and its drainage field. For best results, inspect it annually. The frequency with which a septic tank should be cleaned depends on its size, daily sewage intake, and the number of people it serves.

Unless the tank is large enough to accommodate additional wastes, the use of a garbage disposal will require more frequent cleaning. When the total depth of scum and solids exceeds a third of the liquid depth of the tank, the solids should be removed. With ordinary use and care the tank will probably need cleaning every 2 years. Your local health department may help you locate someone to perform this service.

Because warm weather hastens bacterial action, septic tanks should be cleaned in the spring. The waste material gives off noxious odors and may contain dangerous bacteria. Therefore, it should be disposed of in a manner approved by your local health department. No chemicals are capable of reducing solids in a septic tank to the point where cleaning is unnecessary. Cleansers generally should not be added to the sewage.

Showers

(See "Bathtubs, Sinks, and Showers.")

Skylights

(See "Windows.")

Smoke Detectors

If your new home is equipped with smoke detectors, certain basic procedures will ensure that they function properly in an emergency. Carefully review the manufacturer's literature to familiarize yourself with each unit. Smoke detectors are either battery operated or connected to your home's electrical system. Most battery-operated detectors will continue to sound until a reset button is pushed. Other types will stop automatically when smoke is cleared from the chamber. Check the manufacturer's literature to see which type you have so that you may act accordingly if the detector is accidentally triggered. Periodically test the detector to see if it is working properly.

Different types of detectors will require different care. Follow the manufacturer's recommendations for periodic maintenance. Such maintenance may include replacing the light bulbs, replacing the batteries, vacuuming the unit inside and out, and cleaning it with a cotton swab and alcohol.

Steps

(See "Driveways, Walks, and Steps.")

Stoves

(See "Ranges, Ovens, and Broilers.")

Termites

Termites are easier to bar from a new house than to exterminate from an old one. You should conduct your own inspection in the spring of each year. Look for possible remains of the winged insects. Search the sides of basement or foundation walls and piers for the earthen tubes that termites build to reach the wood above the foundation. Use the blade of a knife to test wood for soundness. If you suspect the presence of termites, consult a professional exterminator.

Toilets

Never flush down the toilet materials such as hair, grease, lint, diapers, sanitary products, and rubbish. Such waste stops up the toilet and sanitary sewer lines. (For unclogging a toilet, see "Drains.")

Cleaning—A variety of commercial cleaners are made especially for toilets. Use them according to the manufacturer's directions, but do not mix them or use them with household bleach or any other cleaning product. And never use them in anything but the toilet.

Leaks—Most toilets have a water chamber, flush valve, overflow pipe, float, and ball valve. If the water chamber appears to leak, the water may only be condensation forming on the outside of the tank and dripping to the floor. (See "Condensation" under "Foundations.") If water leaks into the bowl through the overflow pipe, try bending the rod so that the float will be closer to the bottom of the tank. Flush the toilet, and if it still leaks, the inlet valve washer probably needs to be replaced. If the water trickles into the bowl but is not coming through the overflow pipe, it is coming through the flush ball valve. The connections between the ball valve and the flushing handle may need aligning so that the ball will drop straight down after the handle has been pushed. A worn ball valve or dirt or rust

45

on the ball seat will let water leak into the bowl. If the ball valve or ball seat is dirty or rusty, clean it. If the ball is worn, replace it.

Trimmings and Moldings

Trimmings and moldings, such as baseboard quarter-round, may separate from the floor and leave a small space that will catch dust and dirt. This separation is part of the normal process of settling and shrinking in your home. Loosening the quarter-round or other trim and renailing it in its proper position will remedy the problem. If a small separation occurs at corners or at other seams, it can be patched with wood filler; however, sometimes further settling will bring the pieces together. The filler can be stained or painted to match the molding. A thin piece of cardboard or heavy paper slipped under the molding will protect the floor or rug while you are painting.

Tubs

(See "Bathtubs, Sinks, and Showers.")

Vents

(See "Louvers" under "Attics.")

Walks

(See "Driveways, Walks, and Steps.")

Walls and Ceilings

Your house has two types of walls: bearing and nonbearing. Nonbearing walls may be altered without fear of structural damage, but alteration of a bearing wall must be done carefully to avoid reducing its bearing capacity. All exterior walls are bearing walls. All ceilings are essentially the same in structure, but they are made of a variety of materials.

Interior Plaster and Gypsum Wallboard—Regardless of whether the interior walls of your house are plaster or gypsum wallboard, they should last for the life of your house without undue maintenance. In unusual cases, such as extreme shrinking in framing boards, minor cracks may appear in wallboard or plaster walls. No repairs should be attempted until you redecorate the room. At that time, fill the cracks with spackling compound (available from any paint store), smooth it out with fine sandpaper, and then redecorate the entire surface. Except in very unusual conditions, cracks should not reappear. To prevent cracks wider than half an inch from reopening, apply the spackling compound, then cover the crack with a strip of fiberglass mesh made for this purpose, cover the mesh with another thin layer of spackling compound, feather the edges well, and sand smooth.

Sometimes normal shrinking will cause nails to pop from wallboard. The framing boards and the wallboard shrink away from the nail and leave it sticking out beyond the surface of the wallboard. Popped nails do not alter the strength of the wall, and they should be left alone until you redecorate. Then they should be reset, respackled, and repainted with the rest of the wall.

Unusual abrasions may scuff or indent the surface of plaster or gypsum walls. If this occurs, fill the indentation with two or three applications of joint compound used for drywall taping. Smudges or spots on interior stucco finish may be removed by rubbing it with a fine grade sandpaper (size 00).

Interior Foundation Walls—(See "Foundations.")

Interior Paint and Wallpaper—The interior walls and ceilings of your new home should give you long service if properly cared for. Consult your paint and wallpaper dealer for the correct cleaning compound for painted surfaces and wallpaper. Your dealer can also assist you in choosing from hundreds of possible paint colors and wallpaper patterns when you wish to redecorate or make color changes.

If paint starts to blister or peel, repaint or touch it up immediately to prevent the problem from spreading. If the problem persists, look for the cause, such as moisture penetration through overhead joints or finishes.

Interior Paneling—Interior walls may be paneled in wood, cork, and a myriad of synthetic materials, some of which look like wood. Most of these are stain resistant and easy to clean. Wood paneling may require a special wood cleaner, but some wood for interior walls has been treated or coated so that it is as stain resistant and as easy to clean as the synthetics. Care of these varies with the materials, but most of them can be cleaned with a cloth dampened in a mild solution of detergent and water, followed by a clear water rinse. Check with the supplier of your paneling to learn what is best for your specific wall surface.

Exterior Brick Walls—Brick walls add a special character to a home. Do not expect each brick to be perfect and spaced perfectly. Small surface chips or cracks and slight variations in size and placement are normal and help to create the texture and beauty of brickwork. The mortar joints in brickwork are subject to weathering over the years. When this occurs, the joints should be pointed up (new mortar inserted) to maintain a weather-resistant exterior. This work should be performed by a brick mason.

Glazed tile or bricks may be cleaned with a soap-and-water solution. Stubborn discolorations usually may be removed by gently scrubbing with a nonabrasive household cleaner or a special tile cleaner.

Clay masonry homes may require cleaning by a contractor specializing in this type of work. He or she may use a steam or a steam-and-water jet with a suitable cleaning compound.

Efflorescence—A white powdery substance composed of one or more crystallized soluble salts sometimes develops on masonry walls. It usually can be removed by scrubbing with water and a stiff brush.

Exterior Wood Siding—If your home has wood siding, you do not have to worry about wear. Do not overpaint the exterior of your home because excessive repainting builds up an unnecessary and troublesome thickness of paint which may crack and peel. Where paint is thin, cracked, or peeling, the siding should be repainted to prevent moisture penetration and rot. Siding made of coated plywood or plastic-finished wood may be guaranteed for the life of the house.

Aluminum, Steel, Vinyl, and Other Exterior Synthetic Siding—Many synthetic sidings are guaranteed against cracking, chipping, peeling, and termites for 10 years or more. Most of them resist marring and scarring and are nearly maintenance free. Dirt and fingerprints around doors and windows are easily removed with a mild detergent solution. For other areas, infrequent hosing may be sufficient.

Water Heaters

All water heaters (whether gas, electric, or oil) have a control mechanism to govern water temperature. The dial should be set at 120° F or lower. Your household's individual preferences should determine the hot water temperature. The lower the temperature setting, the less fuel you will use, which could produce considerable savings on your utility bills. Additional savings will result from putting an insulation jacket on the water heater. On gas heaters be sure the air intake is not obstructed. Avoid storing anything near the heater that obstructs the flow of air or creates a fire hazard.

Water heaters normally collect small quantities of scale and dirty water. To remove this material, first shut the water intake valve and turn off the power source for your water heater (gas, electric, etc.). Failure to turn off the power source could cause the heating element to burn out. Then open the valve at the bottom of the heater and completely drain the tank. Open the water intake valve and allow some water to flow through to flush out the remaining sediment. Shut the valve at the bottom of the tank. When the tank is full, follow manufacturer's instructions for restoring heat. In localities with especially hard water, a water softener will reduce the frequency of cleaning.

Temperature and Pressure Relief Valve—Every 3 or 4 months you should check the temperature and pressure relief valve on your water heater to be sure the lever works properly. If the thermostat should fail to operate properly, this valve would prevent a dangerous increase in water temperature and pressure.

Noisy Pipes—If you hear noises in the pipes when the hot water is turned on, it may mean that air or steam is in the pipes. The steam may result from the water being too hot. Reducing the temperature of the water may help. (See also "Plumbing" and "Faucets.")

Water Intake Valves

(See "Plumbing.")

Windows

Your windows may be framed in a wide variety of materials, including aluminum, steel, wood, solid vinyl, and vinyl-clad wood. Wood frames should be painted whenever the house or trim on the house is painted (every 4 to 6 years). Aluminum, vinyl, and vinyl-clad wood do not need painting. Steel frames should be painted with a rust-inhibiting paint. Aluminum can be left to age to a uniform gray. The oxidation (or graying) will protect it from the elements. If you prefer to maintain the brighter new look, a coat of wax will work well. To restore aluminum that has turned gray, polish it with steel wool. However, prevention is easier than polishing.

Skylights—Skylights may leak if the seal breaks. When your roof is being inspected for general maintenance, have your seals, caulking, and flashings around skylights inspected for any cracks or interruptions.

Storm Windows—If your house has double-glazed windows (two layers of glass with a sealed air space in between), you may not need storm windows. In extreme climates, storm windows over insulated glass may be cost-effective for energy conservation. If storm windows are provided with your house, using them will reduce your heating and cooling bills. When exchanging the glass and the screens in the spring and autumn, be sure to clean them both. Many houses in temperate climates do not need storm windows.

Cleaning—If the outside of a window is extremely dirty, use a piece of crumpled newspaper to wash the glass with a solution of equal parts vinegar and water or 3 tablespoons of denatured alcohol per quart of warm water. You may also use a commercial glass cleaner. Lightly soiled windows will usually respond to a solution of 1 cup of vinegar to 1 gallon of water. Apply the cleaning solution with a sponge or lintless cloth, and dry the glass with a chamois or a lintless cloth. A rubber squeegee will speed the drying process. The window frames can be cleaned with a mild detergent solution. (For marble sills see care of marble at the end of "Countertops.")

Minor Repairs—Wood windows may need new glazing compound occasionally. Remove cracked, loose, or dried-up glazing compound, and clean out dust and dirt with a clean dry brush. Replace any missing glazier's points (the small pieces of metal that hold the glass in place). Roll some fresh glazing compound between your hands to stretch it out. Fit it against the glass and the wood with your fingers and smooth it with a putty knife. Oil paint can be mixed with the compound to color it, or it can be painted. For a broken window, remove the remaining glass, all old glazing compound, and glazier's points. (**Warning:** Wear gloves!) For a broken window that is not framed in wood, consult a supplier for advice on replacement.

If a window does not slide easily, rubbing the channel with a piece of paraffin should help. An old candle will do. The same treatment will work for sliding wooden closet doors. For metal doors and windows, use a silicone lubricant.

Miscellaneous Household Tools and Supplies

Tool Kit—You will need a few basic tools and supplies for everyday use in keeping your home in top shape. A suggested list follows:

- ❖ Medium-sized adjustable wrench
- ❖ Standard hand pliers
- ❖ Needle-nose pliers with wirecutter
- ❖ Screwdrivers, small, medium, and large with standard and Phillips heads
- ❖ Electric screwdriver
- ❖ Claw hammer
- ❖ Rubber mallet
- ❖ Hand saw
- ❖ Assorted nails, brads, screws, nuts, bolts, and washers
- ❖ Level
- ❖ Plane
- ❖ Small electric drill
- ❖ Caulking gun
- ❖ Putty knife

Other tools can be rented or purchased as needed.

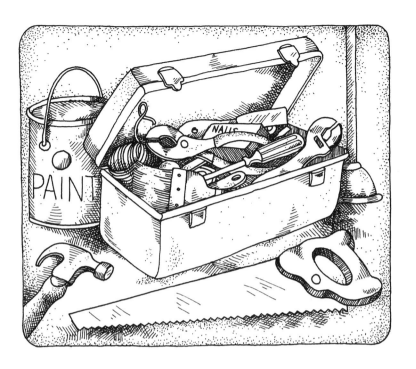

Fire Extinguisher—Every homeowner should buy at least one fire extinguisher. Each member of the family should be familiar with its location and operation. Have it checked annually to be sure it functions properly and is fully charged. Be sure you and your family know how to turn off the electricity, gas, and water in the event of an emergency. Some types of fire extinguishers should not be used for electrical fires.

First Aid Kit—Keep a home first aid kit or first aid materials in a convenient location. Buy and keep with it a booklet on first aid and home safety.

Duplicate Keys—Have duplicate keys made and keep them in convenient places so that small children who lock themselves in the bathroom or other rooms can be freed promptly. When you take a vacation, leave a key with a trusted neighbor. If you forget to attend to something before you leave or if an emergency arises, your neighbor might be able to take care of it.

Annual Checklist

Depending on where you live, most of the items on this checklist will apply to your home.

❖ Check the condition of glazing compound, caulking, and exterior paint. Replace or paint as needed (spring).

❖ Exchange glass and screens in storm doors and windows (autumn and spring).

❖ Inspect the roof for snow damage; repair it if necessary (spring).

❖ Check for evidence of termites (spring).

❖ Check interior paint and redecorate when necessary.

❖ Seed and feed the lawn (spring and/or autumn); plant annuals (spring); do appropriate pruning of perennials (some in spring, others in summer or autumn); rake and compost leaves; mulch perennials that need winter protection.

❖ Remove hose connections and store hose to avoid freezing (autumn).

❖ Keep driveways, walks, and steps free of ice and snow to avoid damage to them and to prevent hazardous walking and driving conditions.

❖ Have your heating system cleaned and repaired if necessary (when not in use). If your unit has an air filter, replace it at least every 3 months during each heating season.

❖ If you have a separate air-conditioning system, clean and change filters as the manufacturer recommends.

❖ Oil motors of appliances as directed in instruction manuals.

❖ Check cords and plugs of all electrical appliances for wear. If necessary, have them repaired or replaced.

❖ Test your smoke detector for proper operation. Be sure to clean the unit (with a vacuum or swab), clean the filter (if any), and replace batteries and light bulbs when necessary.

❖ For security systems, check that the alarm and circuits are in working order; inspect the sensors one by one; and check primary and backup batteries once a month.

❖ Inspect all doors and windows for proper operation and a tight fit. Clean all window tracks, clean and adjust the door thresholds, and check the weatherstripping on windows and doors. Preventing unwanted outside air from leaking into your home will reduce your energy bills.

❖ Check the attic insulation to be sure the entire ceiling area is covered. Check the eaves to be sure the insulation has not blocked the vents. These vents must remain unobstructed to prevent the buildup of condensation and to allow the proper amount of air to circulate in your attic.

❖ Make a careful safety inspection of your home, inside and out, to seek out problem areas before someone is injured.

  ✦ Make periodic checks of storage areas, backs of closets, basement corners, etc., to be sure no oily rags, unvented gas cans, painting supplies, or flammable cleaning materials have been forgotten. These items could be a fire hazard and should be discarded. Many local fire departments will provide free home safety inspections.

  ✦ Check stairs, steps, and ladders for broken or hazardous areas that could cause an accident. Check handrails and railings for sturdiness and reliability.

  ✦ Test all the lights located in infrequently used spaces to be sure they work when they are needed.

  ✦ Check all connections to your electrical system to correct any possible hazards. Replace frayed electrical cords and do not overload extension cords.

Make a detailed checklist of all inspections and repairs required in your home. Leave spaces so that you can record the items as completed. An example of such a list is included in the back of this booklet.

NAHB Builder Members

When you purchase a home built by a member of the National Association of Home Builders, you benefit from building techniques derived from many years of experience and research. Builders who belong to the National Association of Home Builders and the local home builders association in your area are constantly informed of the latest developments in the housing industry. Builders who belong to the National Association of Home Builders stress high standards, provide high-quality workmanship, and give you the best value for your housing dollar.